UNSTUCK

UNSTUCK

MOVING FROM RESENTMENT TO RESILIENCE
WHILE LIVING WITH DYSTONIA

ABIGAIL BROWN

bel esprit books
Dallas | Fort Worth

Unstuck: Moving from Resentment to Resilience While Living with Dystonia

Abigail Brown

Copyright © 2024 Abigail Brown

Published by Bel Esprit Books, LLC
PO Box 821801
North Richland Hills, TX 76182

Cover Artwork: Abigail Brown
Author Photo: Brad Brown
Cover/Interior design: Kent Jensen | knail.com

ISBN: 9798991152808

First Edition: July 2024

To my resilient parents

Brad and Sindy Brown

Who taught me not to give up.

CONTENTS

INTRODUCTION

It happened suddenly.

When I was only three years old, I began suffering from the effects of an undiagnosed case of Rocky Mountain Spotted Fever, which was caused by a tick bite that happened a few weeks prior. My parents took me to my pediatrician, who rushed me to the nearest hospital. There, I was in a drug-induced coma for a week. When I woke up, my muscles were tight, with my arms pulled up to my body. My legs were rigid. I could not move, talk, or swallow. My parents tell me I cried and screamed constantly.

Eventually, I received a feeding tube and was transferred to a rehabilitation center. While in rehab, my speech-language pathologist pointed to the alphabet blocks she was lining up on the floor in front of my wheelchair. She asked me my name and age. My arms were still drawn up to my chest. But with my left foot and great determination, I pointed to the letters spelling out my name and the number three. The therapist asked me my older sister's name and age, as well as my parents' names. I spelled them all.

When they saw that my cognitive abilities were undamaged, my parents felt ecstatic and hopeful about the future. They were told that I would recover within one year so we began a rigorous therapy program with high expectations. For several months, my mom, sister, and I traveled three hours round trip to Oklahoma City, where I would engage in physical, occupational, and speech therapy three days a week. My parents and therapists worked tirelessly.

I relearned how to walk and regained the use of my left hand, but my ability to speak never returned. I'm sure my parents explained it to me the best way they knew how. It's hard to imagine the thoughts that must have been going through my little head, not to mention what was going through theirs.

My parents were only 26 years old.

When I was five, my parents discovered that the brain trauma I had experienced led to the development of dystonia. Dystonia is a neurological movement disorder, which causes muscles to tighten and the body to contort in different ways. Currently, there is no cure for dystonia, although I have undergone numerous surgeries and procedures, like Deep Brain Stimulation and Botox injections, to alleviate some of the more painful and debilitating symptoms.

I grew up learning to communicate with others using several different communication devices. I currently use an app on my phone to talk with family and friends. Growing up I had to have help with everything—getting dressed, showering, going to the restroom, and eating.

I remember the day my mom told me, "I think it's about time you learn how to dress yourself." The first time I tried, it took almost 45 minutes, and that's not counting putting on my leg braces and shoes. From then on, I would pretend that I was in a race with other handicapped kids who had to put their braces on. When I look back, it makes me smile to think I probably won every race.

Obviously, the experiences surrounding dystonia have been life-changing, but the most important event happened when I accepted Jesus as my Savior at the age of seven at a kid's event at church. I prayed in my heart as my mom prayed out loud. That day I entered into a relationship with Jesus. It's the best decision I've made in my life. The Lord has been so faithful.

Can you relate to my story? If so, you are in the right place. I believe the seven-step process I've created can help you move from resentment to resilience, whether you live with dystonia or another disability.

The Britannica Dictionary defines *resentment* as a feeling of anger or displeasure about someone or something unfair. And *resilience* is the ability to become strong, healthy, or successful again after something bad happens.

You will move from resentment to resilience when you have a different response to your past experiences and current circumstances.

James 1:2-3 says, "My brethren, count it all joy when you fall into various trials, knowing that the testing of your faith produces patience."

You may be wondering, "How am I supposed to

rejoice if I'm still struggling to do daily tasks?"

In this book, you'll go through the process of getting UNSTUCK. If God can help me learn how to do this, I know He can and will help you as well. This process will produce the outcome you desire: to live a life of resilience. You can move from a life of misery to a life of joy. It's all up to you.

Will you take the first step?

CHAPTER 1

UNTANGLE PATTERNS OF BLAME

"When I was a child, I spake as a child,
I understood as a child, I thought as a child: but when
I became a man, I put away childish things."

1 Corinthians 13:11 KJV

"What about 'pigeons?'" I whined in my three-year-old voice on the old home movie.

Chuckling, my mom asked, "What does 'pigeons' say, Abbey?"

I lay back on the piano bench and looked straight into

the video camera with a grin. "Children don't trust your parents," I answered.

"Are you sure that's what Ephesians says? It really says, 'Children *obey* ...'"

"'... Children *obey* your parents,'" I repeated.

"'In the Lord ...'"

"'In the Lord ...'" I echoed her, then finished it for myself, "'for this is right!'"

"Right!" My mom cheered.

And then the video clip ends.

Just like that, it is over.

That old home movie always stops too soon. I've replayed the last known recording of me speaking hundreds of times. Every time I watch it, I find myself on the same lonely journey through the "what if" and "why me" valleys. Over and over, I have tried to figure out why God allowed dystonia into my life. It has taken away my ability to speak, to walk easily, to use my arms and hands, and sometimes, my ability to see. Right now, I am typing every word of this book using only my left thumb.

At times, thinking about my losses is almost as exhausting as living with them.

I often picture myself as a physically-able person. Every time I do, I ask myself countless questions like:

What would I be doing today if I didn't have dystonia?

Would I be married?

Where would I live?

What kind of experiences would I have had by now?

How would I be spending my days?

If I focus on those thoughts for too long, I find myself chasing "could've" or "would've" statements into a deep whirlpool of emotions that can take me down for days or weeks at a time. One question leads to another, and before I know what is happening, I am stuck in resentment.

I know that asking God questions isn't a bad thing, but I also know He may never answer some of the questions I have.

Anyway, asking *why* won't change the fact that dystonia greets me like an unwelcome guest each morning. I usually want to stay asleep just a little bit longer because I know as soon as I get out of bed, it will begin. Tightness starts running through my body without my permission. Some days are better than others, but when it's a difficult day—one packed with accidents—I wish I had never answered my alarm clock and pulled my head off the pillow.

No one knows what I face, I inwardly grumble to myself as I get up and get dressed.

Slowly shuffling into the kitchen, I drop my phone. That's a small hiccup for most people, but not for me. When I bend down to pick up the phone, I lose my balance and suddenly ... *SPLAT!* I'm on the ground.

There's nothing like starting the day with a fall, I think, smirking to myself in the silence.

By now, I have figured out there are certain ways that I can get up off the floor without pain. Rolling over to my stomach and getting on my knees, I carefully stand up, take a deep breath, and walk over to the counter to make a well-deserved glass of iced coffee. My morning has hardly started, and I already feel tired.

Does this sound familiar to you? The day is wobbly from the beginning, and you just want to go back to bed. But you know you can't stay in your cozy cocoon forever.

If you're like me, you may have pressured yourself to learn to be happy with a condition that you didn't want. I've tried to convince myself to see the good in my limitations. But the more the dystonia would progress, the more frustrated I became. Over time, I grew angrier and angrier about my teeth-grinding and eye-spasming as I tried to communicate with others. Even simple acts of daily living, like eating and drinking, are terribly difficult for me.

It didn't seem fair, and I wanted someone to blame.

The Resentment Cycle always begins with blame, then self-pity, which leads to frustration. Finally, bitterness sets in.

And bitterness is more crippling than dystonia could ever be.

None of us want to end up there.

So how do we get out of this dreadful cycle? We start by identifying who or what we are blaming.

In the book of John, we read about a man who was paralyzed for thirty-eight years. He felt stuck. He longed to be healed, but he couldn't get into the pool of Bethesda in time, which was understood to have special properties. Whenever the waters started stirring, the first person to get into the water would be healed. Over and over again, the paralyzed man missed his chance.

Jesus walked by the paralyzed man and asked, "Do you want to be made well?"

It seems like the answer would be obvious.

But it wasn't.

The paralyzed man looked up and said, "Sir, I have no man to put me into the pool when the water is stirred up; but while I am coming, another steps down before me" (John 5:6-7).

Do you notice the blame?

Instead of focusing on what Jesus is offering to do for him, the man focuses on what other people are *not* doing for him. He almost missed the gift.

Are we any different?

The Deceiver wants us to think that we can either have dystonia or have a purpose, not both. He would like us to blame every negative circumstance on dystonia. Satan's favorite pastime is watching us play the victim card.

But the Defender invites us to wake up and live abundantly with dystonia. In Isaiah 41:10 He says, "Fear not, for I am with you; Be not dismayed, for I am your

God. I will strengthen you, Yes, I will help you, I will uphold you with My righteous right hand."

If I am going to accept the lovely gift of protection from my Defender, then I need to do my part in receiving what He offers. It's true that I will always wear the jumpsuit of dystonia: twisting, squinting, and jerking day after day. But I also have another suit underneath my "dystonia suit," and it's always with me, too.

It's called the Armor of God.

Our responsibility is to "put on the whole armor of God, that [we] may be able to stand against the wiles of the devil" (Ephesians 6:11). When we don't, we lose the victory and default to victim.

We cannot pick up our heavenly armor while we are still carrying the tangled mess of blame.

I don't know about you, but when I think about untangling something, I picture my dad untangling cassette tapes for my sisters and me when we were kids. I also think about untangling jewelry. Whether you are untangling cassette tapes or necklaces, there is always a point when it seems like a lost cause. But with a bit more time and attention, the knot eventually gives way.

The same approach is required when we start untangling our patterns of blame. At first, it may feel hopeless. But identifying your patterns will begin the process to reach freedom.

What kinds of blame swirl around in your head every day?

My own tangled thought patterns involve:

- blaming dystonia for my not being able to drive.
- blaming people for how they talk to me or look at me.
- blaming my parents for not reading my mind and knowing exactly what I want.
- blaming the circumstances that brought dystonia into my life.
- and blaming God for not healing me.

At times, those tangles can be overwhelming, keeping me in victim mode and preventing me from truly living.

That's a truth that was made all too real to me when I was recovering from a bad cold last week. After a couple of absences, I finally returned to the children's Sunday School Class where I volunteer. The kids greeted me with excitement.

"Miss Abbey, welcome back!" One of the girls exclaimed.

I hugged her and sat down to take roll. Everyone was chattering happily about the fun craft we were going to do that morning.

As class began, I realized that the character trait we were talking about that month was *initiative*. The negative thoughts that had been beating me up the past week started up again. Lies I assumed were true kept pulsing in my head:

You're not qualified to say anything about initiative.

You aren't able to help others.

You're an inconvenience.

This time, I was aiming the blame at myself, the easiest target of all.

While I was distracted by my tangled thoughts, the girls in the class were making their craft: funny glasses out of colorful pipe cleaners. As they were finishing up, one of the girls asked if I were going to make any glasses.

I put my fist beside my nose, my personal sign for *No*.

A few minutes later, the teacher asked me if I'd like

her to make me some silly glasses.

Again, I smiled and signed, *No*.

Then the teacher asked the girls, "Raise your hand if you want Miss Abbey to have some glasses."

All the little girls in the class quickly shot up their hands.

As I watched them raise their hands with great joy, I sensed the Lord saying, *See? Others want you to join the fun.*

Just like the paralyzed man by the pool of Bethesda, I had almost missed the gift.

You might be doing the same thing.

Today, I invite you to put on a new pair of glasses so that you can see your life differently. Let's call them glasses of gratitude. Instead of viewing everything through the lens of blame, let's identify those patterns and get them out of the way so we can finally see our purpose.

REFLECTION TIME

1. Where do you most often place blame? Circle all that apply.

God	Family	Friends
Strangers	Dystonia	Doctors
Medicine	Church	Culture
Your Body	Time/Age	Society
Other:		

2. What's the real problem? Ask the Holy Spirit how He wants to heal you. Circle what you're struggling with.

Entitlement	Unforgiveness	Bitterness
Discontentment	Lack of Joy	Anger
Hopelessness	Lack of Peace	Self Pity
Self-Sufficiency	Comparison	Envy
Other:		

3. What are the most common negative sentences that fill your thoughts?

1. _____

2. _____

3. _____

4. _____

5. _____

4. Do you want to be healed of these beliefs? If Jesus were to walk by and ask you that question right now, would you be willing to let Him untangle your patterns of blame? Write out your prayer below.

_____

_____

_____

_____

_____

_____

_____

CHAPTER 2

NOTICE THE BLESSINGS GOD HAS GIVEN YOU

*"I will be glad and rejoice in thy mercy:
for thou hast considered my trouble; thou hast
known my soul in adversities."*

Psalm 31:7 KJV

The night before my sister got married, I woke up at four in the morning and couldn't go back to sleep. It was my first time being a bridesmaid. I knew my duty was going to look different from the others. Physically, I had been preparing for months, trying to build up my stamina to stand on the stage with the bridal party.

As I stood still for long periods of time every day, my mind had stopped focusing on what was happening for my sister and had started focusing on what *wasn't* happening for me. I struggled to be happy for my youngest sister and her soon-to-be husband. I fought with the thought, "This isn't how it's supposed to go. I am older than she is so I should have gotten married first."

It didn't seem fair.

In my dark hotel room on the morning of the wedding, worry set in. *Would I fall while walking down the aisle? Would I burst into tears during the ceremony? Would the pictures be good?*

Trying to relax, I thought I'd listen to the Bible on my phone app. Before long, I was calming down and halfway-listening to Psalm 31. That's when I heard verse seven in a new way: "I will be glad and rejoice in Your mercy, for You have considered my trouble ..."

The words of Psalm 31:7 were refreshing. To me, the most significant part was, "For You have considered my *trouble* ..." Although King David was going through different circumstances than I am, he knew that the

Lord had considered his trouble.

Notice how your perspective can change when you replace the word "trouble" with *dystonia, job, mate, health, year,* etc. The Lord considers what we go through from day to day.

The God of the universe actually notices and cares about the details of my life. If He can pay attention, then surely I can, too.

A few hours later, the sun rose, and I texted my sister an encouraging message before the excitement began. As I slipped on my elegant burgundy dress and fixed my hair, I felt peace for the first time in a long time. I was able to stand up on the stage and watch my beautiful sister get married. And I didn't fall one time that weekend. (What a miracle!) There were so many blessings to notice.

God had helped me to focus on the good again. I don't like admitting it, but there are times when I can be bratty and dive into self-pity. I can become discontent at the snap of a finger. Sometimes I am blinded to the blessings the Lord has given me.

For example, last year, I bought new bedroom furniture. I was very excited when it arrived. Then, only a month later, I walked into my room, sat in my comfy swivel chair, and looked at myself in my new vanity. I glanced at my new bed, with its new bedding and the adjustable mattress I've always wanted.

But instead of being content, I thought to myself, *I'm not independent. I'm still living with my parents.* That thought stayed on replay in my mind all week long.

One morning during that week, I was sulking around, grumbling to myself about how confined and limited I am, living with this annoying disability that's not going away. As I continued to rant in my mind, a question popped up: "What am I making *independent* mean?"

Sensing I was onto something significant, I started writing in my journal, "Being independent means doing things on my own."

It seemed obvious that I should make a list of things I can do and things I can't do on my own. Guess which list was longer? The list of what I *can* do!

My "I can" list consisted of:

- I can get out of bed.
- I can walk.
- I can feed myself.
- I can dress myself.

- I can bathe and go to the restroom by myself.
- I can take my medication.
- I can order food and clothes online.
- I can send encouraging texts to friends and family.
- I can communicate with others.
- I can fix certain meals.
- I can write.
- I can paint.

And my "I can't" list contained:

- I can't drive.
- I can't fix some meals or cut food into bite-sized pieces.
- I can't always take certain medications by myself.
- I can't provide a place to live alone.

When we choose to notice the blessings in our lives it makes us feel better. But I'll admit, it can be hard to find reasons to be thankful in the circumstances of this disability, especially when I fall. Recently, I lost my balance in the crowded foyer of my church. I fell on my knees so hard that I couldn't put weight on my left leg. I winced in pain, stunned by how fast the people around me pulled me up and helped me over to a chair to sit.

My face felt hot as I heard someone say, "I'll go get her parents."

Gulping down tears, I tried to calm myself. My knee throbbed, and I could barely even type to communicate, "I'm fine."

"Your knee is bleeding," a kind lady said.

I pointed to my purse, and she saw there was a bandage she could put on my knee. If I had been alone, I would have had to figure out how to open that wrapping with my crab-like left hand. I hate to think how long that would have taken.

While it's not pleasant to fall in public, I am thankful I had people who cared to stop and help. We all need people to stop and help us when we physically fall, but we also need people to help us when we spiritually fall.

When we spiritually fall, it's not as noticeable as when we physically fall. We can hide our spiritual falls. On the days when we descend into frustration or disappointment, people will not know to run over and apply bandages to our hidden heart wounds.

Do you feel unseen in areas of your life? Maybe you're like me, and you stay home for the majority of the week.

I have felt unseen many times. Each time I do, the Lord sends me something special to show me that He still considers my trouble.

It happened again after church recently. I was standing near the doors, telling people goodbye as they left. I've learned this is something I can do while I wait on my dad to pull up the car.

As I was waving and hugging people, a sweet, soft-eyed truck driver in a light tan suit walked up to ask in the gentlest voice, "Can I pray for you?"

Before I even gave him a thumbs up, he placed his hand gently on my left shoulder and started praying quietly enough so only I could hear. As he was praying, I felt my face flush, and tears rolled down my cheeks.

"God," he prayed, "I thank you for giving Miss Abbey the strength to get up and come to church today. While we as a church family may never know what she does to be here, You do. Give her strength for this week and bless her in all she does."

It's times like these when I can't help but feel seen and loved by God. He notices me.

So I am making it my passion to notice Him, too.

REFLECTION TIME

1. Set a timer for 5-15 minutes. Notice as many of your blessings as you can before the timer goes off.

_____

_____

_____

_____

_____

2. How many things can you put on your "I can" list?

_____

_____

_____

_____

_____

_____

3. In what ways can you make gratitude a habit, incorporating it into your day?

CHAPTER 3

SPEAK TRUTH TO YOURSELF

"Let the word of Christ dwell in you richly in all wisdom; teaching and admonishing one another in psalms and hymns and spiritual songs, singing with grace in your hearts to the Lord."

Colossians 3:16 KJV

It's soft taco night at our house, and I'm sitting down to have dinner with my family around our oblong dining table. Everyone starts making their tacos. My mother makes mine and cuts it up. As she places the plate in front of me, she sees it's one of those days.

Conversations start, and I want to listen, but I also have to concentrate just to balance myself in my chair. My right arm swings in the air like a bull rider. I stab a bite with my fork and wait for my tongue to stop thrusting and cooperate. By the time I am finally able to open my mouth and swallow the food, I look down and realize I only have fifteen more bites to eat.

Eventually, everyone finishes eating, and I am the only one still sitting at the table. Tears roll down my cheeks as I continue trying to eat. Oh, how I wish meals were easy for me.

The everyday task of eating is where several of my thoughts became toxic. Over and over, these sentences repeat in my mind:

It's not fair.

This is frustrating.

Why does eating have to be hard?

No one understands what I go through.

Can't anything be easy?

Even though I didn't speak the words out loud, saying them to myself in my head had the same effect of creating solid, set-in-stone beliefs.

We have all heard the old adage, "You are what you eat." But Proverbs 23:7 warns us, "as [a person] thinketh in his heart, so is he." In other words, you are what you think. Stop right there for a moment and ask yourself this question: If you were guaranteed to become a living illustration of the thoughts in your head, would you like what you see?

Let's take a look at the thoughts I just voluntarily revealed to you and see what they are producing for me.

It's not fair. — When I think something isn't fair, I create more unfairness. How? Because I am not being fair with myself or God. I become the only person around the dinner table who is not enjoying life in a peaceful home on a beautiful day. Instead of focusing on the fact that everyone in my immediate family is alive and together for a meal, I focus on my limitations the entire time. That is not fair to me because I deserve to be treated well and not self-criticized for my disability. And it is not fair to God who gave me a lot of wonderful things to appreciate, but I am not thanking Him for any of them at that moment.

This is frustrating. — When I think something is frustrating, I create more frustration. How? Because I keep trying to do things I expect I should be able to instead of letting go of my expectations and taking a deep breath. Holding onto expectations that are not being met is always frustrating. I could use my brain and heart to be more creative and imagine alternate solutions instead of using them to maintain my expectations. It would be better for me to assume that there is always a way, and that I can always figure it out. That would empower me to keep going.

Why does eating have to be hard? — When I think eating is hard, I create more hardship in eating. How? Because doing anything without enjoying it is a hardship! I don't think about the lovely smells and tastes. I don't find ways to participate in the conversation. I only dwell on my mechanical process and try to hurry to keep up, so I make meals harder. One idea to make meals easier would be to just be okay with being the last one at the table. I could decide to like it. I could slow down and make meals easier by enjoying them on purpose.

Eating dinner with family or friends can still be

challenging, but I can enjoy the little things. For example, my mom made roast, potatoes, and carrots last week (a good ol' Brown favorite). I don't know why my mouth was having trouble swallowing that night. When this happens I try to listen to the conversation and not focus on the bite of food that I'm currently trying to consume. If I rush myself, I spend all my energy looking at how long it is taking for me to swallow each bite. Then I become even more tight.

On that particular night, I was listening to my dad tell us about his day, and out of the blue I accidentally let out a loud *WOOH!* It surprised me and startled my mom, which made me laugh! That allowed me to break the tension in my body just enough so I could swallow. On a challenging day, one bite at a time is a victory.

No one understands what I go through. — When I think no one understands, I create even less understanding. How? Because I do not try to understand others. And I do not seek to understand myself better, either. As a result, I miss the obvious and all-important tool of my mind. It is the one part of me that still works at full speed. And I could have been using it to change the results in my life the entire time. Maybe the worst part about thinking this thought is that I overlook the opportunities to find the people who actually *do* understand what I am going through: other people with dystonia. I do not intentionally seek them out or try to build relationships in that community.

Can't anything be easy? — When I think nothing is easy, I create more situations that are not easy. How? Because I don't do the easiest thing of all: change my thoughts.

Two years ago, I decided to invest in myself and start talking things out with a Christian life coach. At first, it was hard for me to accept what my coach said. She told me that what I think and say to myself really does affect how I feel. Not only did I hesitate to believe that was true, it was a challenge for me to even name or describe how I was feeling. Over and over, she would ask me how I felt about something, and I would shrug my shoulders. I didn't know how I felt.

It took a year of coaching to soften my heart toward this new process. The first year we were patiently exploring my feelings. Even when I came up empty-handed, not knowing how I felt, we were making progress. It wasn't until the second year of working together that we started to move forward with my thought patterns. Week after week my heart became softer, and eventually I could see the change my renewed thoughts had made in my life.

For example, one of the statements I would repeat when I'd fall was, *It happened again*, and I'd mentally beat myself up. After talking it out with my coach for a few sessions, I decided to start telling myself, *Sometimes falls happen*. It is a small and simple shift, but it doesn't lead to the same mental and emotional pain.

It makes a difference—sometimes over time, sometimes right away.

This shouldn't come as a big surprise. The apostle Paul told us how important our thoughts were in the book of Philippians, when he wrote, "Finally, brethren, whatever things are true, whatever things are noble, whatever things are just, whatever things are pure, whatever things are lovely, whatever things are of good report, if there is any virtue and if there is anything praiseworthy—meditate on these things" (4:8). An interesting note: He was in prison when he wrote this. Obviously he had learned that when you are stuck in an unwanted place or powerless position in life, you still have authority over what you think.

Why would Paul put such emphasis on our thoughts? Because Jesus did. In Luke 6:45, He tells His followers, "A good man out of the good treasure of his heart brings forth good; and an evil man out of the evil treasure of his heart brings forth evil. For out of the abundance of the heart his mouth speaks."

Your thoughts and feelings are the treasure of your heart. They are being stored up as words you will speak. And the words you speak are seeds that will produce a harvest in your life. So it's in your best interest to speak truth.

Even if you cannot use your mouth.

When I was three years old, and we learned that my ability to speak would not return, our family started learning American Sign Language and made up some unique signs so I could communicate. I learned the sign for the word *frustrated* really fast. It wasn't long before I was putting the back of my left hand in front of my mouth and nose to communicate *frustrated* again and again.

Maybe you cannot use your mouth to speak truth over yourself, either. Words can come out through writing, sign language, and grunts or groans. They can even come out in laughter or tears. Every form of communication counts. When you realize that, it makes you slow down and become aware of what you are communicating.

One of my earliest discoveries of the spiritual power of words happened when I was in third grade and I learned the song *Did You Ever Talk to God Above* in junior church. It reminds us how God is everywhere and we can talk to Him as a friend. The Lord knows my thoughts, and I don't have to pray out loud for Him to hear what I'm saying. I started singing it in my head at night when I couldn't go to sleep because I was grinding my teeth. I didn't realize it at the time but I was learning how to encourage myself by singing songs in my head.

I love Colossians 3:16: "Let the word of Christ dwell in you richly in all wisdom; teaching and admonishing one another in psalms and hymns and spiritual songs, singing with grace in your hearts to the Lord."

Like Paul and Silas sang to the Lord in prison in Acts 16, the Lord also invites us to sing in our confined bodies.

It's one thing to speak or sing truth to ourselves, but we should also be letting others speak and sing truth to us. That's why every morning I put on some praise music to start my day. I also listen to my Bible and a podcast or two each day.

You may have struggled with thoughts like I did and felt ashamed and hopeless. You may think you can never transform your thinking from negative self-talk. I'll explain how to do that in the next chapter. For now, your first step may be to share these unhelpful thoughts with one person you trust. You become courageous with yourself when you bring what you've been thinking into the light.

And when you become courageous with yourself, you will start being kind to yourself.

REFLECTION TIME

1. Identify the unhelpful thoughts you think about most often.

_____

_____

_____

_____

_____

_____

_____

_____

_____

_____

_____

_____

2. Look closely at the sentences you've just written and circle the ones that are a lie the devil is hoping you will belicve.

3. Now spend some time searching for Bible verses that will counteract those lies with truth. Write down each truth and speak it over yourself.

CHAPTER 4

TRANSFORM YOUR THINKING

"And be not conformed to this world:
but be ye transformed by the renewing of your
mind, that ye may prove what is that good, and
acceptable, and perfect, will of God."

Romans 12:2 KJV

I knew it would happen, just not this soon.

On a routine appointment to receive injections in my brow, mouth, and eyelids, my doctor said,"Botox won't be helpful to you much longer."

All the color drained from my face in an instant. *Without the Botox, what would relieve me of the unrelenting tightness of dystonia?*

Seeing my concern, he told me I would be a good candidate for a surgery called Deep Brain Stimulation (DBS). He explained that DBS is a procedure where they put electrodes in the brain (I'd have to be awake during that part). Then there would be another surgery to put two electrical remotes under the skin on my chest to control the electrodes. He said the neurosurgeon in Oklahoma City had done several of these surgeries on Parkinson's patients, and it had helped them.

"It's really quite simple," he said, matter-of-factly. I couldn't help wondering if he would still call it "simple" if *he* were the one undergoing the surgery.

I had a lot to consider. The upside of such a risky operation would be that it could help restore mobility to my left hand, balance to my walking, and freedom from my neck and back pain. Also, I could potentially stop getting more than two dozen Botox shots every 90 days.

The key word being "potentially."

The more the doctor spoke, the more questions filled my mind: *I thought DBS only worked for people that had generalized dystonia, not secondary? Has this neurosurgeon ever operated on a person with secondary dystonia before? What's the percentage of success for this surgery among people with dystonia?*

My doctor thought it could help ten to 20 percent of my body. "Of course, there's always a chance the surgery might not have a beneficial effect. If that's the case, you could have the electrodes removed."

A ten to 20 percent improvement was at stake. One might argue that such a slim margin might not be worth it. To have two electrodes placed in your brain and two remotes with rechargeable batteries implanted in your chest is a massive undertaking for such a small return. Still, I was willing to go through all of it to have a better quality of life ... even if just a little bit.

After that appointment in October, I put off thinking about the procedure for weeks. No one could make the decision on my behalf. At 22 years old, it was up to me. But any time the surgery came up in my thoughts, I would push it out of my mind, not wanting to make the final choice. I reasoned that it would be at least a year or more before it would happen, and I could take my time to think about it.

Soon those plans would change.

Three months later, I went to my usual Botox appointment, and my doctor asked if I had made a decision about DBS. I told him I was still considering it. I knew the surgery could change my life in many ways if it worked. But even if it did work, it might be a long time before we saw results. My doctor would have to program the remotes in my chest, and that would require a time of trial and error. It could last a year or more.

I told my doctor that the main reason I was postponing my decision was the fear of being awake while the electrodes were being placed in my brain. I could not even let myself imagine what it would feel like when they were drilling into my skull.

Later, the neurosurgeon assured me that it would be similar to filling a cavity at the dentist. There would be pressure but not pain.

Pain or no pain, it still sounded gruesome to be awake and aware while someone was exposing your brain tissue. Even so, I decided to move forward with the surgery. Living with dystonia during that time was limiting. I was falling more, and there weren't many things I could do with my left hand. I could only use my pointer finger and thumb to do everyday tasks. From my perspective, DBS was a risk worth taking.

In my journal , I wrote about how I was feeling.

At a glimpse, circumstances may seem like a fog clouding your vision. Blinded and unable to see what's ahead, Satan slithers through your thoughts, pulling you down an undesired path. Ask the Lord to arrest your thoughts and guide them towards things above.

As we waited for the surgery date, God calmed my fears again and again by guiding my thoughts to things above. In Psalm 92:4, we read, "For You, Lord, have made me glad through Your work; I will triumph in the works of Your hands."

My first triumph came quickly.

From the time I had announced my decision to have the surgery, I was praying and asking the Lord to make it possible to have it while under general anesthesia.

A week later, the nurse called and said the doctor would be able to do the surgery while I was asleep.

I was excited when my mom texted me the news!

But the thrill didn't last long. I was still worried about the possibility of the surgery not working. A month before the surgery, I wrote a poem entitled, "He Paved The Way."

Stepping into the unknown is like
Walking into a dark room,
Fearing that you might fall.
As your eyes adjust to the darkness,
You can start to make out shapes.
Reaching out to finally turn on the light.
This is how I feel.
I am still trying to find the light.
I am scared.
What will happen if I turn on the light?
What will change?
What will it feel like?
It is best to not see what the light will convey,
And trust in Him who paved the way.

Are you noticing a trend? My thoughts go up and down. They are helpful to me sometimes and unhelpful to me other times. Helpful thoughts keep me in a good mood; unhelpful thoughts can take me to a painful place.

Circumstances affect my thoughts, and my thoughts affect my circumstances.

That would be enough of a struggle. But the truly challenging part for anyone who lives with a disability is that *their* thoughts are not the only ones that can be problematic. Their primary caregiver is dealing with a lot of helpful and unhelpful thoughts, too.

Recently, I saw how unhelpful thoughts can have an impact on my primary caregiver, my mother.

It all started because I had been keeping a little secret to myself for weeks: I had begun having bathroom accidents at home. Sometimes, I would have to clean up the mess and do a load of laundry two or three times a day. I was embarrassed and didn't want to tell anyone. I just wanted to deal with it on my own. I was afraid if I let my family know, I would end up wearing adult diapers. And I certainly didn't want that.

Each time I'd have a bathroom accident, I'd think, "I should at least tell mom." But every time I worked up the courage to tell her, I'd talk myself out of it.

Just like I kept putting off thinking about the DBS surgery, I kept putting off letting her know about the increasing bathroom accidents. But thoughts will not go away, just because we try to push them away.

This secret pattern of cleaning up multiple times per day went on until one holiday weekend, I couldn't hide it anymore. My family had decided to eat at one of our favorite Mexican restaurants and then go shopping. We all were excited to go somewhere other than the hospital. Only one month before I had undergone the DBS surgeries, and there had been many grim trips between the hospital and home.

But everyone's mood was upbeat and fun that night ...

Until I had two bathroom accidents in the span of two hours.

"Has this been happening for a while, Abbey?" my mom said with slight irritation in her voice. As she helped me clean up, I could tell how exhausted she was.

I signed yes and started crying.

"Stop crying!" she snapped. Then she started sobbing and said, "Something like this always happens. I'm so tired. We can never just have a normal day."

Finally, the mess was clean, and my parents decided we had better head home. Disappointment loomed as we left the outlet mall. We drove in silence.

When we finally pulled into the driveway, my mom apologized and told me that she was frustrated with the situation and not me. I understood.

She is the same person who cheers for me when we leave a Botox appointment, saying "Yay! You did it again! You did a good job holding still this time! It can't be easy, especially getting shots in your eyelids."

I smile back at her in the rear view mirror, while thinking about what the rest of my life might look like: *taking medicine, getting thirty injections every three months, recharging the batteries in my chest, living with the ebb and flow of tightness.*

Recently, it was like the Lord tapped me on the shoulder to interrupt my unhelpful thoughts and ask, "Have I not been faithful to you before, Abbey? I know it might be hard right now with all the changes but remember I am here with you through it all. You can depend on Me."

Yes, of course I can. Remembering that He is dependable is a helpful thought, indeed.

During seasons of uncertainty and fear, I am reminded of Hagar in her time of need. When she was sent away by Abraham and struggled to survive in the desert, she called God *El Roi*, meaning the *God Who Sees*. Genesis 16:13 reads, "Then she called the name of the Lord who spoke to her, You-Are-the-God-Who-Sees."

Her circumstances didn't change right away, but her awareness of the Lord's presence did.

The same God who saw Hagar also sees us. He knows what we'll face and will give us peace and comfort as we go through every valley of uncertainty. As you're reading this, you might be facing a circumstance you're unable to control. If so, may I encourage you not to dwell on the outcome of the circumstance and to dwell on the presence of the Lord, instead? I know it's easier said than done, but it has helped me to shift my attention to things I can control. I can always control how much attention I give Him.

It also helps me to look around and focus on other people's circumstances. How can I help them with prayer or words of encouragement? While I am pouring hope into others, there are times when no one is pouring hope into me. Sometimes the only encouragement I get is in my day-to-day walk with God. Notice how it all comes back to His presence and how much of my attention I am giving Him? Listening to His Word, writing down what He says about me, and playing uplifting music will have an effect over time. It's in the consistent little routines of life where I see spiritual growth.

Helpful and unhelpful thoughts are important to notice, whether they are about serious subjects, like brain surgery and bathroom accidents, or about lesser topics, like messy desks.

If you could see my desk right now, you would notice I have a devotional book I haven't opened in years, and on top of that is my Bible. I also have three journals: one is pink and purple plaid, another is pink and says "Stay Fabulous," and the third one is mint green. Next to my journals, you'll find my gray sign that says *You are loved* in white lettering. Oh, and my iPad is stacked sloppily on top of it all. My laptop sits in the middle of my desk. I have pens and miscellaneous items in the pen holder. On the other side of it is another journal, and on top of that journal is my iPad stand. Beside it, I have remotes for various things.

My desk is a mess to say the least. It has looked this way for months. I could take time to organize it, but I just don't want to.

The statement, "I just don't want to..." can creep into

my mind very easily. And as long as I keep thinking that I don't want to, I can keep piling things onto my desk. In the same way, if I think "I just don't want to ..." when it comes to analyzing my thoughts, I can keep piling unhelpful thoughts on top of one another until my mind is as messy as my desk. If I don't acknowledge that certain thoughts are lies, then how will I start believing statements that are true? I must choose to make time to write or type out the anxious and unhelpful thoughts that keep bogging me down and barging in.

For example, Miss Easier For Them has crashed so many parties in my mind. A few years ago I drew what I imagined this 'thought' may look like. She was a stick figure that pulled luggage.

I bet you didn't know Miss Easier For Them has ten sisters! There's Miss Easier to Be an Artist, Miss Easier to Be a Writer, Miss Easier to Be Single, Mrs. Easier to Find a Husband, Miss Easier to Leave Right Away, Miss Easier to Travel, Miss Easier to Live on Her Own, Miss Easier to Have a Conversation, Miss Easier to Make a Meal, and Miss Easier to Get Things Done.

Unhelpful thoughts about life being easier for others have been my go-to beliefs for years. They can still arrive at the party of thoughts going on in my mind. I'm just more aware when they pop by for a chat. I have to remind myself that while it may look easier for others, I really don't know if it's easier. I'm only assuming that from a distance.

In the end, the best thing for me is to focus on what the Lord has called me to do.

I've also created new, helpful thoughts for myself, like Miss Get 'Er Done, Miss Fully Functional Lady, Miss Problem Solver, Miss Born to Do Challenging Things, and Miss Ponder and Discern. Trust me when I say, they are a lot better company.

You can become more aware of your thoughts, too. You don't have to keep engaging with the lies that constantly nag you. It's okay to acknowledge that dystonia is challenging, but don't let every thought get a free pass to rule inside your head. You can transform your mind. This is what 2 Corinthians 10:5 means when it urges us to bring "into captivity every thought to the obedience of Christ."

For me, when I became aware that I had thoughts that weren't helping me move forward in life and that weren't pleasing to the Lord, I asked God to forgive me and help me start thinking better thoughts towards Him, others, and myself.

Because our minds are the most important place to get unstuck.

REFLECTION TIME

1. Give a few of your most common unhelpful thoughts a name.

_____

_____

_____

_____

_____

_____

2. Use the space provided to draw stick figures of those "friends" who usually crash the party in your mind. What are they wearing or carrying?

3. Now give names to the helpful thoughts that you want to invite over more often.

_____

_____

_____

_____

_____

_____

CHAPTER 5

UNDERSTAND THAT GOD IS WITH YOU IN EACH SITUATION

"Draw near to God, and he will draw near to you."

James 4:8a (NKJV)

During one memorable session with my life coach, I was struggling to communicate. We live in different states so we meet weekly on Zoom, and she asks me challenging questions, while I answer by typing in the chat or using a few hand signs. On that particular day, my facial muscles were so tight that I couldn't see what I was typing.

The harder I tried, the more I messed up. She waited patiently. My frustration was reaching its peak.

Seeing my predicament, she asked me to pause.

"I know this situation is not what you want, Abigail. Just stop and breathe for a minute." After a few seconds, my coach continued, "All right. Let's switch the question. How about considering some ways that dystonia is working in your favor. How is it serving you?"

What?!

That question was worse than the first one. I threw my head back in anger and let out a sigh of irritation. As I started to reply in the chat, my eyes squinted uncontrollably, and my teeth ground together.

Dystonia is working in my favor?

I don't think so.

We made it to the end of the coaching call with a few empty words in the chat. I was only trying to fill time. I didn't mean a single one of them.

As usual, my coach invited me to reflect on that question in my journal until our next session. By the end of that week, I had actually made a detailed list of how dystonia was working for me, but I began second guessing what I'd written. For instance, one of the statements I typed out was:

"Living with dystonia has given me opportunities to reach out and get to know all sorts of people."

Deep down, I believed this statement was true, but that week I just wasn't feeling it. I preferred to indulge in my negative emotions while I was getting over a cold. I don't know about you, but dystonia seems to get worse when I am sick. It takes twice as much energy to stay positive. I felt terrible, and I knew I was writing down words to make my coach happy, not because I believed them.

The wheels of my mind continued to turn on her question day after day between our coaching sessions. Late one night, I asked the Lord to help me understand how dystonia is working in my favor. I just didn't know.

And this is what the Lord placed on my heart:

I can do the impossible, Abigail. Remember, I'm the One who works through your weaknesses. My Grace is sufficient for you, Abigail. You are not alone in this. I am for you. Dystonia is working in your favor, and it always has been. Have faith like Noah, Moses, David, and many others you grew up learning about.

Your name means "source of joy," and that you are. But I am the Source of your joy, and I'm the only One who can satisfy your longings.

I was aware of His presence that night, and I had a peace come over me. It's hard to explain, but at that moment, I began to believe I could do anything with dystonia. I had memories flood my mind of His constant abiding presence and faithfulness.

He is with me when I choke on medicine.

He is with me when I'm super "gritty," and when my entire body aches from being tight, and my neck throbs in pain.

He is with me when I'm disappointed because my Botox appointment gets rescheduled.

He is with me when I cry out in frustration.

He is with me when I choose to turn on praise music and hum along.

He is with me on both the good days and challenging days.

I have a choice to abide in his presence moment by moment, knowing the Lord has a purpose for me.

Has there been a time in your life when you have felt

the presence of the Lord? He is the God of all Comfort (2 Cor 1:3). No matter what you are facing, you can choose to abide in His presence moment by moment, knowing the Lord has a purpose for you.

And when that is hard for you, just know that I am somewhere out there, relying on Him to help me do the same thing. In order for us to be aware of our purpose, we might have to turn aside from distractions, like Moses did.

In Exodus 3 we find Moses watching his father-in-law's sheep in the desert. Suddenly, the angel of the Lord entered into a bush. Moses was confused. The bush appeared to be on fire, but the fire was not destroying the leaves or branches.

Moses must have looked around his flock of sheep, and when he saw he could step away from them for a moment, he said, "'I will now turn aside and see this great sight, why the bush does not burn.'

So when the Lord saw that he turned aside to look, God called to him from the midst of the bush and said, 'Moses, Moses!'

And he said, 'Here I am'" (Exodus 3:3-4).

Moses decides to "turn aside" from what's happening

in his life and enter into the Lord's Presence. When I read this passage, I asked myself the questions: *Do I notice or turn aside to come toward the burning bushes in my life? Am I aware of the Lord's Presence?*

Not always. There have been times when I knew the Lord wanted me to do something specific, but I didn't obey right away because I didn't want to or felt like I didn't have the time.

For example, recently I went to a concert with my parents and some friends. We got to the concert early to get a good view. After we were in our seats, we waited for a long time. I could tell the lady beside me was very curious about me, but I acted like I was doing something important on my phone.

I just ignored her. And she let me.

During the concert intermission another lady *in front of me* looked back, smiled, said hello, and asked my name. I smiled and then looked down at my phone, considering if I should say anything back.

Then that familiar debate began to rage in my mind and heart: *Should I respond? Will it take too long? Will she be annoyed if she has to wait? Is she just trying to be polite and doesn't really want an answer?*

Once again, I ignored someone. I knew I should've told her my name when she asked me. I just didn't want the conversation to be awkward while she waited for me to respond by typing it out ... so I did nothing. Looking back, I can see how not answering her question is already awkward.

But the lady in front of me wasn't like the lady beside me. She didn't give up so easily. Guess who she asked because I didn't answer?

My mom. And my mom looked at me and said, "Do you want to tell her?"

My face flushed as I heard the lady say, "Oh, I thought she couldn't hear me."

I quickly started typing, "My name is Abigail." Then I handed her a pamphlet I wrote about myself, explaining why I communicate the way I do.

Her interested expression was a delightful surprise.

After the concert the lady in front of me turned back around, and we embraced as she said, "One day in Heaven, I can't wait to talk to you more and hear your beautiful voice sing."

As we exited the auditorium, I had to wipe my tears away so I could see where I was going in the crowd of people. It is a rare treasure for me to find connection through conversations. For most people in our fast-paced society, chatting with me is just too slow. I don't want to hold people back, so entering into conversations as a nonverbal person makes me feel uncomfortable. It doesn't take long before I can tell other people feel the same way.

But when you come into a relationship with the Lord, you have full access, and you can communicate with Him any time of day. You are never holding Him back. In fact, He loves to listen, no matter how long it takes. Even though He is the Creator of the universe, we have permission to approach Him. The Bible assures us that, "we do not have a High Priest who cannot sympathize with our weaknesses, but was in all points tempted as we are, yet without sin. Let us therefore come boldly to the throne of grace, that we may obtain mercy and find grace to help in time of need" (Hebrews 4:15-16).

Sometimes I don't take advantage of this wonderful gift.

Like the two ladies at the concert, I have often ignored the Lord. But He doesn't give up. He has continued to pursue me even when I've picked up an offense against

Him that I knew I shouldn't. It is one thing to bring questions to Him, but it is another thing to hold an offense against Him. Offenses will pull you apart. Questions will draw you closer.

There was a time recently when I questioned again why the Lord had allowed dystonia in my life. I was in the middle of writing this book, and I needed to get unstuck, yet again. As it turns out, staying unstuck is a daily battle.

I was trying to work on this chapter and kept asking the Lord which stories I should share. My parents had gone on vacation so I had the house all to myself for ten days. Of course, a productive writing week was all planned out in my head.

This is the perfect opportunity to write because I'm not even tight! I could get several chapters written!

Or so I thought.

As the week progressed, I'd sit down to write, but everything I wrote felt forced. So I'd stop and walk around inside the house, listening to a Christian meditation podcast called *The Revelation Wellness Podcast*. The topic the instructor was talking about that week was the presence of God.

I didn't want to stop listening, so I walked around the house from the kitchen to the dining room, into the entryway, through the living room, and then I'd be back in the kitchen/bar area. I did five laps that way, then rested long enough to have energy for five more laps.

At the end of that day's episode, I was in tears. I could see the image the instructor was describing. Jesus was looking at me and holding both of my hands. It normally takes time to pry open my left hand because three of my fingers have atrophied shut. But when I imagined Jesus reaching out to hold my hands, He didn't hesitate to take them in His, and He held them until they relaxed.

Immediately, I remembered a sermon I had heard a few weeks before. The guest preacher had taught out of Philippians 4:6, reading, "Be anxious for nothing, but in everything by prayer and supplication, with thanksgiving, let your requests be made known to God."

And wouldn't you know that the preacher talked about how we need to let go of the situations that the Lord has allowed in our lives and give them to God. Believe me, I have done that plenty of times while living with dystonia. But I had picked up the unanswerable questions again, and I sensed that Jesus wanted to pry my hands open so that I could let go.

You might be thinking, "Abigail that's great for you, but I've prayed and prayed, and the Lord still feels very far away."

I have felt that way, too. Sometimes the inward screams that can't be heard by anyone are welcomed by the only One who can take it and doesn't abandon us. So while it may seem like He's not listening or paying attention, He is very aware of what's happening in your life. The Bible is filled with good promises like Deuteronomy 31:6, which says, "Be strong and of good courage, do not fear nor be afraid of them; for the Lord your God, He is the One who goes with you. He will not leave you nor forsake you."

That promise, along with all the rest, will continue to be true until the Lord returns. And until He does, He sends His Presence to comfort us when life doesn't make sense.

REFLECTION TIME

1. Identify your level of awareness of His presence. Where are you on a scale of 1-10?

_____

_____

_____

_____

_____

_____

2. In what ways can you increase your awareness of His presence?

_____

_____

_____

_____

_____

3. Describe a time when you vividly felt His presence.

CHAPTER 6

CRUSH COMPARISON AND COMPLAINING

"Do all things without complaining and disputing, that you may become blameless and harmless, children of God without fault in the midst of a crooked and perverse generation, among whom you shine as lights in the world,"

Philippians 2:14-15 NKJV

"Abbey, you're going to have to type it out," my mom said, trying to help me get used to my new five-pound communication device with 128 buttons.

Whimpering like any 8 year old would, I reluctantly started typing, using only my left pointer finger.

The sound of beeps filled the room, and the computerized child's voice said, "I'm ... so ... different."

There was nothing left to say, as I cried in my mom's embrace.

At age eight, I had started noticing that disability made me different from other kids. I compared the way I communicate to how others communicate. At the time the percentage of kids speaking with Augmentative and Alternative Communication (AAC) devices seemed small. It felt like I was the only person who used one. I walked with a walker that had a mount so it could carry my AAC device.

There is a special, symbol-based language system for the AAC device called Minspeak. For example, a picture of a girl pointing to herself, then a picture of a wanted sign, and then a picture of an apple meant "I want to eat." I memorized the many sequences quickly, and my vocabulary grew each year. It was almost like I was learning a second language.

From the walker to the heavy device to the sound of my computerized voice, it was painfully obvious that I wasn't like other kids. So I started a miserable habit of comparing and complaining. As I grew bigger, so did my tendency to focus on others in frustration, no matter if their circumstances were better ... or worse.

For example, when I was ten years old, my family went to listen to a presentation by a man who was born with no arms. His message was both interesting and inspiring. My mother had hoped that it would help me feel less isolated to see that he struggled to do ordinary tasks, such as eating with his foot.

However, when we got home my mom asked me what I thought, and I typed out, "At least he can talk."

Looking back, I have compassion for the younger me. I was thinking about myself and my problems, like any other fifth grade girl might. I wasn't thinking, "Wow! I'm so thankful I have arms and hands that can do so many things in life!"

Instead, I focused on how easily he talked instead of noticing his other difficulties.

In other words, what *I* didn't have stood out more than what *he* didn't have.

Stop and read that again.

What I didn't have stood out more than what he didn't have.

Isn't that what we all do? I overlooked *his* lack and thought about my own. I didn't even consider if he wrestled with the insecurities of living with no arms. It's quite possible he did. I was too young to realize that the unifying factor for us probably wasn't disability, but insecurity.

The more I compared my differences instead of looking for similarities, the more I felt alone.

It would be four more years before I met someone who communicated with an AAC device. He lived with cerebral palsy and worked as an AAC consultant. He was in the neighborhood helping a boy learn how to use his new communication device.

The boy, who was much younger than I, was a new acquaintance for our family. On the day the AAC consultant visited their house, the boy's mother called mine and exclaimed, "Please come over, if you can. There's a guy here you all need to meet!"

When I saw him, I was shocked. It was the first time I observed another person's hands and fingers moving like mine. His face drew up in a smile like mine, as well.

It was at that moment I knew I couldn't be the only one who communicated differently. And for the first time, I felt a wave of hope.

The next day I was scheduled to speak at a seminar for physical, occupational, and speech therapists. I don't remember what I said to the audience that afternoon. But I vividly remember meeting a girl around my age who was in a wheelchair. She also communicated with an AAC device mounted in front of her, but she operated it by using software that responded to her eye movements. When she looked at a particular button, a computerized voice would speak for her. We communicated for a short time right before the seminar started, and my heart was happy to make a new friend.

After feeling isolated for so long, it was impactful to meet two AAC users in two days. Discovering that I wasn't the only one who was nonverbal was a revelation, and I'd like to say that my attitude changed after those wonderful opportunities to meet others who communicated like I did. But it didn't. Even though I couldn't imagine having to "type" everything with my eyes, the newness of the revelation wore off quickly, causing me to forget what a gift my life is.

Discontentment seeped into the area of my heart where comparing and complaining were already situated and comfortable. Like any teenager, I was bogged down in wanting to be accepted.

Teenagers want to blend in. To be typical. Normal. Average. Part of the crowd.

Needless to say, that is not the case when you use a sippy cup.

That's right, during my teenage years I still drank out of a green or pink sippy cup that had handles on the sides. I became more and more self conscious of this as I got older. I remember going to thrift stores and looking for lightweight cups with handles. Mugs were too heavy. Other cups were not the right size. If it was too tall, then I might have to tip the cup back too far, and my shirt would get soaked and stained.

I wanted a cup that wasn't so eye-catching and didn't make me look so young. One day my mom was at a thrift store and found two light weight red cups with thin plastic handles. I was so excited when I saw them! I loved that they had one handle I could easily grasp. Plus it looked normal and held more liquid than the other cups I used.

But contentment evaporates quickly. It wasn't long before I forgot why I thought it was such a great cup. I was still getting looks when I went out to eat with my family. Each time the waiter would assume I was a kid and give me a kid's menu, I became aggravated. I was doing everything within my control to act like a teenager.

The weeds of comparison and complaining were scattered throughout the flower bed of my mind. Untended, these thoughts surrounding my appearance and the way I had learned to live with a disability started growing waving in the wind. It was as if the weeds were saying, "Don't pay attention to the flowers. Look at me!"

Thanks to technology, communication is much easier now. I use an app on my phone, and I find myself blending in with everyone else who is on their phones for one reason or another. Yet there are still times when I compare and complain about how I am so much slower in every way. If I am not careful, comparison can take hold of my life, causing me to limit myself, and become hyper-focused on what others have accomplished.

In John 9:2, the disciples compare themselves to the

man who was born blind, asking Jesus, "Who sinned, this man or his parents, that he was born blind?"

At first glance, it may not appear that this was an act of comparison, but I believe they wanted to know why they were able to see, and he wasn't. Surely it was because someone in his family had done something wrong.

Right?

For a moment, the disciples may have felt superior.

But Jesus replies gently, "Neither this man nor his parents sinned, but that the works of God should be revealed in him. I must work the works of Him who sent Me while it is day; the night is coming when no one can work. As long as I am in the world, I am the light of the world"

(John 9:3-5).

And, just like that, Jesus crushes their comparison, turns the focus around, and reminds them to get back to work.

It's Jesus who shines light on the sin of comparison and complaining in your life and mine. He confronts us with the truth. And then, like a potter, He molds and shapes us into beautiful masterpieces of His Grace. God created us in His image, yet we are all uniquely different.

My parents tried to help me see that I wasn't the only person who lived with disabilities or communicated differently. I'm thankful they taught me to think about others, even though sometimes I didn't really want to.

When we start comparing ourselves to what we think other people think about us, it becomes harder to identify who we are comparing ourselves to. As Christians who are saved by grace, we know we are adopted children of God and joint heirs with Christ. That means we are valued and treasured more than what we can comprehend. We should compare ourselves only to Jesus, not to other humans. Obviously, we can never measure up to Him. But that is the point. He chooses and redeems us anyway.

Comparison can create conflict within your heart and mind when you are trying to be content. I tried and failed at contentment many times while depending on my own strength. I was striving, striving, striving. However, true contentment and peace can only be found when you stop striving and abide in Jesus. It's only when I trust and depend upon the Lord that I can find satisfaction and fulfillment in life.

Before Jesus went to die on the cross, He told the disciples in John 15:5, "I am the vine, you are the branches. He who abides in Me, and I in him, bears much fruit; for without Me you can do nothing."

The word *abide* means to dwell, remain, be present, to be held or kept.

You can come to Jesus feeling let down and crushed with disability, and He'll take your disappointment, despair, and the things that can't even be put into words. He'll remind you that He never fails, and His Word will stand forever. He will never leave you or abandon you. He has created you to live an abundant life.

There comes a time, though, when you have to examine your life and ask yourself, "Am I truly content with my life with dystonia? Am I living abundantly?" I know it's really easy to pretend you're content. For a pretty good chunk of my life, I acted like I was blessed living with dystonia. For years I had used default phrases like: "Dystonia is a gift," "I'm not a victim of dystonia," and "Dystonia is a privilege." These are all things I've *wanted* to believe but deep down I didn't believe them at all. Once I started admitting that I wasn't really content or living my life abundantly, I became open to choosing a new thought that would help me move on as I continued to live with dystonia.

It's common knowledge that when you plant a seed of any kind of plant or tree, the seed-breaking process is done in the dark. We can't physically see the seed break and roots start to form. Yet we know that when we water the soil of the plant, it will eventually grow. It has to get the nutrients it needs.

The same is true when you start thinking different thoughts. You can plant the seed of a new thought in the soil of your mind, but it won't begin to grow until you give that new thought the nutrients it needs.

For instance, when I would see my younger sisters or my friends getting their driver's licenses, I'd think, "I would have my driver's license if I didn't have dystonia." Or when I would see my friends graduate from college, I'd think, "I would have gone to college if I didn't have dystonia." Or when I would see an author online promoting her book, I'd think, "I would finish my book faster if I didn't have dystonia."

Do you see how many times I bring up dystonia? A funny thing happens when you compare, blame, and complain. You stay the same while your thoughts circle the drain. It can be a challenging process to stop if you aren't aware that you are doing it.

My coach helped me recognize the habit of focusing on dystonia and create a plan so I could crush the cycle of comparison.

She asked me, "In ten years, what thought would you like to think about dystonia? The thought you choose represents a rose bush that will bloom and flourish over time. You need to plant it now," she explained.

With hesitation, I typed out, "In ten years I'd like to say, "I'm living *joyfully* with dystonia."

"Sounds good. So how about in five years? What thought would you like to think about living with dystonia?"

I typed out, "I'd like to be living *all right* with dystonia."

"Now, what do you want to think about dystonia today? This thought is the seedling you'll be protecting and watering in your mind."

I looked at my coach for a second, then typed out, "I live with dystonia."

It was a simple statement that I started saying to myself multiple times a day. At first, when I said this statement

I'd cry because it discouraged me. This was because I was focused on the word "dystonia."

But the key word in that sentence is "living" not "dystonia." I'm living! I'm a Child of God. I am a daughter. I am a sister. I am an aunt. I am an artist. I am a writer. I am a communicator. I am a friend. I am a church member. And so much more! Now that's something to get excited about!

My perspective changed in the moment I realized that it was possible to embrace life living with dystonia. And all it took was a three-step process of growing a new thought. You can try it for yourself by choosing how you want to feel in ten years. Then back it up to the five-year mark. And finally, begin with a seedling thought that you can start nourishing today.

Jesus illuminates the sin of comparison and complaining in your life, urging you to embrace His grace and transformation. Just as He worked to reveal God's glory through the blind man, He continues to mold you into vessels of His grace, guiding you away from comparison and complaint and toward a life filled with His light and love. As you abide in Him, allow His truth to reshape your heart and mind, enabling you to reflect His grace and beauty to the world around you.

You can cooperate with the Master Gardener by watering all those brand new beliefs based on light and love.

Keep at it. Better thoughts will grow.

He promises they will.

REFLECTION TIME

1. Identify who you are comparing your life to.

_____

_____

_____

_____

_____

_____

2. List ways comparison and complaining have affected your life negatively. Write a prayer to the Lord asking Him to uproot the weeds of comparison and complaining.

_____

_____

_____

_____

_____

_____

3. Make a list of "I am" statements and declare who you are in Christ.

_____

_____

_____

_____

_____

_____

4. What would you like to think about dystonia in ten years? What about in five years? And finally, what would you like to think about dystonia today?

_____

_____

_____

_____

_____

CHAPTER 7

KNOW YOUR PURPOSE

*"The steps of a good man are ordered
by the Lord: and he delighteth in his way."*

Psalm 37:23 KJV

I enjoy riding roller coasters. When I was a kid, my family went to an amusement park in Ohio called Cedar Point. This park had one of the tallest and fastest roller coasters in the world at the time—Millennium Force. I was nine years old and barely tall enough to ride on it, but I felt ready. While waiting our turn to ride, I remember seeing the coaster zipping by at a speed I had never experienced.

My leg began shaking as the roller coaster worker

started securing and pushing the lap bars down on each of the riders. My emotions were on a roller coaster, too. I wavered between smiling one second, to pooching my lip a little, to smiling once again. Eventually, the ride began to move forward.

"Are you ready for this?" My dad said as we started going up the blue track.

Click, click, click, click, click...

When we were almost to the top of the first hill, I raised my arms, ready for the drop. My dad grabbed my left wrist and shook it as he exclaimed, "Here we go!"

The ride lasted only a few seconds, then the cars halted and slowly rolled back into the loading area. Everyone on the ride reacted with excitement. I had a big grin and signed "love" by crossing my arms into an X and placing them over my heart. We got out of the car and headed toward another ride. Speeding off in my power chair, I imagined going 93 miles per hour like the roller coaster.

What fun that would be! I thought.

At nine years old, I was fearless.

However, I was not as confident just ten years later. Why do we feel more and more afraid as the years go by? The more I imagined what I'd like to do with my life, the more I worried and felt fearful. As a nineteen year old, I had the most valuable tool in the world: ample amounts of time. How would I use it?

It had been years since I had taken art lessons. I had stopped taking them when I was 16 because it was challenging to try to draw and paint with my eye spasms. So I decided to take a break for a few years as I learned to adjust. But after I graduated high school, I started messing around with painting again.

At first, I painted a lot of flowers. But by the time fall rolled around, I really wanted to learn how to draw and paint pumpkins. My mom found a college age art student who was learning how to be an art teacher, and we were overjoyed. She came to our house one afternoon to give me a lesson on pumpkin painting. I already knew what I wanted the background of my painting to look like. So I decided to paint it before she arrived. The background consisted mostly of yellows mixed with white and some orange. Then, I sat out the two pumpkins that my mom had used as decoration around the house.

By the time the college student arrived, the background was dry and ready to go. I shared with her my desire to learn to draw and paint pumpkins. She knew exactly where to begin. We each opened our sketchbooks to practice drawing the pumpkins on the table before us.

Her drawing looked wonderful, of course, and mine looked like the work of a beginner. Eventually, I drew a sketch that I was happy with and transferred it onto the background I had painted hours before. To fill in my sketch, I mixed up lighter orange for the base of the pumpkin and added bright orange strokes so I could create some depth. I tried doing the same thing with the olive green pumpkin, but I didn't have enough yellow to make the olive green color I saw. So I just used the grass green color I had available and added red highlights. When we finished for the day, I was satisfied. I decided to make it one of four notecards in the fall collection I created over the next year.

As my interest in painting grew and I saw how prints of my original paintings made such beautiful notecards, I started envisioning a future as a creator. I also began writing on my blog which at the time was called *Going Through Trials with God*. As a nineteen year old, I started writing to explain my life with dystonia in hopes of one day writing a book. I started taking writing courses and interacting with several Christian writing communities.

The more I got to know people in the writing groups, the more I realized I wasn't alone. We all struggled with some of the same feelings of inadequacy and doubt.

Maybe you can relate to the desire to add value to your life and community by using all of the extra time you have been given. Your contribution will truly begin when you recognize the Lord created each one of us for a purpose. He has not only given you talents you can use to make a living but He has also given you spiritual gifts to serve and help others better know Him. These spiritual gifts, found in Romans 12:6-8, include: exhortation, giving, mercy, prophecy, serving, leading, and teaching.

How will you use them?

As believers, we are called to use our spiritual gifts to tell the world about Jesus. In Matthew 28:18-20, Jesus announces the Great Commission, and tells His disciples that He has been given authority over both heaven and earth. He instructs them to go out and make disciples of all nations, baptizing them in the name of the Father, the Son, and the Holy Spirit, and teaching them to follow His teachings. Jesus reassures them that He will be with them always, until the end of time.

But as disabled believers, can we also obey the Great Commission?

Yes, you and I can obey the Great Commission by following what the Bible teaches us. One way I've learned to do this is to go about my life creating things, whether it's creating conversations by texting, creating content for my social media accounts, creating a meaningful note, or creating a beautiful painting. When anyone asks how I do it, I am not ashamed to tell them: It's all because of Jesus.

This life I have been given is to be stewarded, or managed well. I'm continuing to learn how to take care of my time. That can be a challenge. For those of us living with dystonia, we can't always predict how much energy we will have when we get up in the morning. But we know ourselves pretty well, don't we? We can tell when we're pushing ourselves too hard, and when we want to throw a pity party and just be plain lazy.

Yes, I said it.

Because I've been there, my friend. There are times when I just want to "check out" and not do anything because I'm enjoying the freedom of not being as tight that day. Sometimes that's okay, but other times I know

I'm capable of doing more. I'm capable of spending meaningful time with my family. I'm capable of doing chores around the house. I'm capable of taking a friend out to eat. I'm capable of being a listening ear to a friend who needs to talk things out. These are just a few ways we can spend our time well and be good stewards. If we're honest, we are usually capable of doing more than we admit.

The point is that we must be honest with ourselves about when it is rest and when it is waste. For instance, my relationship with God is a crucial part of my life, but when I'm in pain, and my body is tight, I have learned to give myself permission to stay home and watch my church services on livestream. So give yourself grace and permission to do what you're able to do. And the moment you feel strong enough, get connected to the lifeline of your local church.

The Lord desires to do so much more than just communicate with you in the privacy of your heart. He also wants to communicate with you in a public setting with other believers.

How often do you attend your local church? Having a church community that can encourage you spiritually can help your walk with God. It's in this environment where you can also serve and encourage others in the Lord.

On a recent Sunday morning, I was running behind schedule. I rushed to drink my ice coffee and then went back into my room to slip on the gray leopard print dress I had picked out the night before. Looking in the mirror I could see obvious tension from the pain I was experiencing in my neck. Sighing, I debated whether I should go or just stay home for the morning.

Then I thought to myself, *Seeing the girls in my Sunday School class always makes my day. You've already gotten this far, Abigail. Just keep getting ready.*

Little did I know that the Lord had a wonderful surprise waiting at church for me.

Moments after we arrived at the building, I headed back to the classroom to greet the girls as they walked in the door. Twenty minutes into the class time, while my neck was still throbbing with pain, my allergies started acting up. I began to sneeze uncontrollably. After class, I continued to sneeze. By that point I was not only in pain, I also was exhausted.

Then, before I made it into the main service, I ran

into a precious lady who thinks I'm deaf.

Exclaiming to all who would hear, she said, "This is my buddy!"

Then she eagerly tried to communicate with me, using hand signs as she talked. Looking at her with grace, I decided to just sit with her during the morning service. I slid into the middle of the pew beside her and asked the Lord to strengthen my body and calm my allergies.

I wanted to cry my eyes out during the service several times that hour. The music was uplifting to my soul as we sang, "He Giveth More Grace" and "My Anchor Holds." That day my pastor was continuing his series in the book of Hebrews, preaching out of chapter four. Verse twelve from that section of scripture reads, " For the word of God *is* living and powerful, and sharper than any two-edged sword, piercing even to the division of soul and spirit, and of joints and marrow, and is a discerner of the thoughts and intents of the heart."

I gulped down tears as the pastor said something to the effect of, "You and I have a God who knows us so deeply, and He will take care of you during your hardest circumstance."

At the end of the service, I made my way out of the

sanctuary and headed to the restroom so I could let out all the emotions I was feeling during the service. I knew if I didn't do it then I'd burst into tears talking to someone else. Just then, a teenage girl came into the restroom and said, "Are you Abbey Brown? Yes I think you are! You might not remember me, but I was in your fifth grade Sunday School class six years ago. I just wanted to tell you that you made a profound impact in my life. I just wanted to thank you."

Shocked by what she said, I hugged her and began crying again, as I quickly got my phone out to communicate with her more.

What a blessing to be reacquainted with that beautiful young lady, I thought on the drive home from church, slowly turning my head side to side to stretch my aching neck. I felt grateful I had made the effort to go to church that day. It wasn't easy, but it was worth it.

The Lord is intimately acquainted with the challenges and joys that await us each day.

As I enter the twenty-eighth year of living with dystonia, I know there will be setbacks and tightness and pain and more falls. But even in difficulty, I have learned that it's possible to serve the Kingdom. Recently, the

Lord reminded me once again that He sees my mundane faithfulness and endurance. He eagerly desires to journey alongside me, guiding me deeper into His boundless love and grace.

In Philippians 3:14, the apostle Paul speaks of pressing forward toward the goal for the prize of the high calling of God in Christ Jesus. This verse highlights the importance of living a resilient and purposeful life as a believer. Even amidst life's unexpected twists and turns, the Lord's guidance remains a steadfast anchor for you, precious daughter of the King. When the journey ahead seems filled with uncertainty and confusion, His presence offers you the strength and assurance to continue trusting in Him.

Hold fast to the truth that His plan for your life is filled with purpose and meaning. Embrace the journey with confidence, knowing that He is with you. So continue boldly walking in your purpose, experiencing continual transformation into the image of Christ.

REFLECTION TIME

1. Identify your talents and gifts by making a list.

2. In what ways can you partner with God with the things you just listed?

3. As you reflect on the faithfulness of God in your own life, how will you continue moving confidently in your purpose?

ACKNOWLEDGMENTS

The journey to writing this book has been a long one. I am forever grateful for the love, prayers, and patience that my dad and mom surrounded me with. From the long talks to the words of encouragement, you both knew I could do it.

To my amazing sisters, Alicia, Anna, and Aimee—Thank you for all the texts and FaceTime calls filled with encouragement and laughter during this time.

To my friends, Hannah David, Anita, and Rachel Armstrong, and my church family—Thank you for covering me in prayer and celebrating with me each time I finished a chapter.

To my extended family members—Thank you all for your prayers and encouragement as I began my writing journey. I love you all so much!

To my writing friends in the Anointed Writers

coaching group: Cherie Nichols, Kristina Frazee, Amanda Mook, Cyndy Gusler, Maggie Fackler, Jenifer Cabaniss, Annie Dueck, Melissa Dossey, Mary Jackson, Cheri Gresso, Michelle Brumgard, Janine Preuss, Kristine Crumb, Melodie Kenniebrew, Sandra Gosch, and Kay Nell Miller—Many thank yous for your weekly encouragement, prayers, and support to keep writing.

To the team at Bel Esprit Books—Thank you for this publishing opportunity.

To my book coach and writing mentor, Nika Maples—I'll be forever grateful that the Lord intersected our paths five years ago. Thank you for spurring me on to keep writing what the Lord had placed on my heart.

ABOUT THE AUTHOR

Abigail Brown has been living with dystonia since age three. She enjoys one-on-one conversations and getting to know others better. She is the founder of Silent Inspirations, a creative studio that offers colorful stationery and home decor based on her original artwork. When she isn't writing or painting, you'll find her listening to audiobooks, connecting with friends, spending time with family, enjoying iced coffee, or learning something new about marketing on social media. Abigail lives in Stillwater, Oklahoma, where she wrote this entire book with her left thumb.

To Order
Abigail's
Greeting Cards

SCAN HERE!

Connect with Abigail

@abigailbrownwrites

Join our community and connect!

Stay encouraged with Abigail's latest posts and updates. Don't miss out!

abidingwithjoystudio.com

Scan here to join

www.ingramcontent.com/pod-product-compliance
Lightning Source LLC
Chambersburg PA
CBHW070726130626
46553CB00005B/2175